Catharsis

Jean Bodin

[handwritten dedication]

für Daniel

mit herzliche Güte

und freundschaftliche

Zuneigung von

April 2013

Catharsis

Decomposition at a Distance on the Record
or
Sleep's Murderer Black Sun

The Hard Way Out
or
The Man and The Satyr

Motility Operon Resurfaced
or
There is No Room for Parasites and Idlers

Jean Bodin

edition lulu/2012

©Jean Bodin 2012
Edition lulu 2012
ISBN-13: 978-1-300-64076-9
Layout: Henrico Jr.

Illustrations by the author.
Set in Linotype Avenir.

Did this Path have a Heart

or

How to Die in the Most Inspiring Pose

*

I was not Hamlet. I did not stand at the shore and talked with the surf **Blabla**, the ruins of Europe in back of me. I had to exist within the ruins and under the poisonous skies. I would not be able to look God in the eye, said the kid to the recruiter. It asked itself only one question: does this path have a heart?

It was **Wolftime**. I had to run from both its pain and consequences. The regime's aim was the "decomposition" of people. Decomposition meant blocking people from acting. It meant paralyzing them as citizens by convincing that everything was controlled. It meant the relent-

less application of a quiet coercion leading to compli-
ance.

**

To be nobody but yourself under a utopia which is do-
ing its best to make you everybody else, the New man –
means to fight the hardest battle which any human being
can fight. Destiny is no matter of chance, it is a matter
of choice. Most of us craved a meaningful picture of the
world and our place in it, an identification of the good
and the evil, and an assurance that in the end the good
(i.e. people like ourselves) will triumph. The fall of the
Wall was such a victory. We made our dream come true.
Now was the time to plant flowers and orchards and have
seven kids.

Wolftime was the opiate of the secular materialists, an
apocalyptic creed which filled the chosen with assurance
of their righteousness and election. But the vast major-
ity of whom had no intention whatsoever of living any-
where other than outside the walls, where they enjoyed
the freedom and prosperity that subsidizes their beliefs.
Their Hamlet was never ours.

***

Their New man pretended to be selfless, learned, healthy and enthusiastic in spreading the ideology.

"New", "young", "vital", "ideal" were pivotal keywords for the breed of Informal Informers (IM). Adherence to **Wolftime** doctrine, and individual behavior consistent with that regime's prescriptions, were among the crucial traits expected of the New man. Destruction was both inevitable (i.e., the removal of the old and corrupt) and desirable (i.e., cathartic, purifying, unifying, and ennobling). Among the major traits of the New man was selfless collectivism. Means and methods were en-acted in a process of culturally stripping the individual naked and atomizing him so he became defenseless and mouldable by the state in each and every corner of social life. The city had no sun.

****

The next step was the "nationalization of time" through central planning. Through the instituting of "the plan", the State attempted to control and manipulate the very concept of time. All human life existed and continued through the dimensions and durations defined by the plan for **The Land Around**. **Wolftime** tried to set and change the boundaries of "past", "present", and "future" by accelerating, shortening, and modifying the temporal horizons within which all economic and social activity were made to confirm. How to reject Telesian doctrine, asked once a monk. **Sleep's Murderer Black Sun**, was the answer.

*****

Finally came "ideologization", the process through which the regime attempted to fill the content of the men's minds and influenced the language and the thought pattern of "the people", in whose name the leaders undertook this grand scheme. How to die in the most inspiring pose? Fear, intimidation, and terror practiced by the secret police secured the suppression of opposition. Philosophia sensibus demonstrata?
It was not Hamlet on the shore, but Don Juan in the bed, who did know, for what to care: does this path have a heart? If it does, the path is good; if it doesn't, it is of no use. **Decomposition At A Distance On The Record** is a selection and formulation of alternatives. It is not an understudy for clones.

HUH

iv

1 Decomposition at a Distance on the Record

or

Sleep's Murderer Black Sun

Chorus in a threesome
IM (inofficial cooperator) Tomasso
The Poet
Gargantua
Wolftime 8 May 1945 - 9 November 1989
The land around

1.1 No Heart Lives Grandly in its Silence

That to him
social and moral hypocrisy were
a thorn in his flesh and just in the same way

the forces that rule the individual,
his drives,
possession by dark as well as bright passions–
did not leave him any peace.

Life
you are a perfect driver,
bliss, roaring of storms, delicateness of pre-
      cious oil.

But in case
you would like to obtain
more information about me, please turn to
one of those present.

You are at liberty
to provide further information about myself.
      Of course
you too are cordially invited.

Stipulated is, in due course,
the deployment of a couple of men for practi-
      cal advanced professional development.

Ah, you are acquainted with our structure. Talk
now
About reproduction.

1.2 Dysmoron

You have made clear to me our responsibility
assignment. I also know your concept. Of course
you too are cordially invited. No woman
will be mated with a man before she has reached
her nineteenth year of life. And a man
may sire before he has exceeded his twenty-first year,
or
beyond this, in as much as he
is of a cool disposition. Before this time,
only few
are allowed to handle women,
however, only infertile or pregnant ones, so that they
are not
forced to seek unnatural ways out. By the way,
so that this subject will never again come up between
us...

I told Tomasso: you need
not have any fear that I will ask you about the party
or other things. What he has thought before, is vorbei.
Older women and civil servants
take care of the pleasures of love of those who are too
         rapturous
and are being importuned all too much, depending on
         whether they
came to know about it, secretly approached by them,
         or
whether they noticed it on the exercise courts. Or in
         the party year of apprenticeship.
However, permission will be issued
by the highest-ranking civil servant for reproduction af-
         fairs
the senior doctor,
who himself is subordinate to the triumvir "love".
As far as we are concerned, we would not have
Shouted this topic from the rooftops. Those however,
who abstain from cohabitation until their twenty-first
         year of life,
and even more those who do so until their twenty-sev-
         enth,

are feted at public assemblies
through honors and songs. I was never in them.

1.3 Whoever Disowns You, May not Shoulder and Cuddle Disaster

They may rebuff it, giving it,
like stone crushers confer to stones, the shape
     of a wall.
Because, in the manner of the old Spartans,
during the exercises all, men and women,
are completely naked, the civil servants,
who are invigilating, recognize who is capable
     of procreation and who
is incapable of cohabitation. Measure for Mea-
     sure.
It depends on physical disposition, and on
who matches up best. The query
is out already. I faxed it right away. Only after
     that
they devote themselves, after the bath, to the
     procedure of love.

That's what
I had hoped, in fact. Large and beautiful wo-
     men
are only joined with large and hearty men,
fat women with gaunt men.
Do you see any new reason why Tomasso
is suddenly in such a hurry? And slim women
     with
strong-bodied men, so that they balance each
     other
successfully. I'll be in touch. I even believe
it's burning.

1.4 Wildly They are Standing Straightened Up, Among Each Other

Who transforms treason into love, betrayal into

following, fear into courage, sycophancy into
     cooperation,
egotism into altruism? Those will be discussed

individually later. Initially, anyway, everything
     is supposed to remain unaffected,
except that we should coordinate distribution.
     In the bed-chamber
there are beautiful canvases of famous men,
     which the women
look at. Thereupon they cast their glances
     through the window
to heaven and ask HIM, may he
endow them with a hearty offspring. So long,
then. You will hear from us. Things will hap-
     pen.
You will sleep in two separate chambers until
     the
hour of intercourse. Provided that we have
     found
agreement so far. Then, however, rises the
war dress, and opens both doors from the out-
     side.
So that with us an immediate readiness for ac-
     tion is a given,
as soon as our technology has been made up-
     to-date. The astrologer and the physi-

cian
determine this hour; they endeavor
to hit the time when Venus and Mercury, to
the east of the Sun,
are in a favorable house, with good aspect
to Jupiter, as well as to Saturn and Mars. If
one could agree,
I don't see anything to prevent us to go the
whole hog.
Initially, anyway, everything is supposed to re-
main unaffected,
except that we should coordinate distribution.

1.5 Erasure From Above Brouhaha

In order to make trousers from this. It is
considered a severe offense if the procreators
do not, for three days before intercourse, ab-
stain from any maculation and any
bad deed. The guards and the teachers,
all of them informants, have, as a result of
their heavy cogitation,

only weak drives and are not fully involved
    with
their mental abilities; therefore, because they
    are always
brooding over something, they are able to
    breed only weakly offspring. For that
    reason
special measures are applied here: these learn-
    ed
scouts are joined with fat women of gentle
    manners. The party joins the cadres
from the party machine, often hot-tempered
    and without character,
with female comrades who are by nature
lively, hearty in coping with life and
beautiful like the 8th of May.

1.6 The Established Well Interpreted

Life is expecting all those of us who
love and compile political-operative assess-
    ments of

circumstances. Who love the wild fragrance
of sea and mint. Again and again questions.
About the efficiency and intensity of co-oper-
        ation
with the inofficial cooperators (IM). The plan-
        ning target
that it salvages between the breasts. Number
        of hits,
duration of hits, maintenance of hit rhythm,
rate of utilization of conspiratorial flats. So
        that they are not
forced to seek unnatural
ways out. What's your position towards
the operative informative value
of the processed information,
voice that forms people?

(German song / singing / canto / chant)

(End)

2 The Hard Way Out

or

The Man And The Satyr

Lamentations
A Chorus of 15

2.1 "There is your phrase", he said.

Her adversaries are the chief, her enemies prosper

For four days they hiked the desert, sweltering in the afternoon and bitter cold at night, sleeping in villages, searching each house and hole they crossed. They had anticipated opposition, but they found instead a conspicuous, almost eerie, absence of military-age men. "It's like when you turn on the lights, the cockroaches all dis-

appear," Folsom said one afternoon. "When you turn off the lights, they all come right back out."
No insurgents, only traces of them everywhere.

Stay updated

> Intellect
> Can not
> Feelings
> Will not
> But the soul
> Wants you to live
> A living death.

Epochal pomp

> No one is sure
> Where to turn
> Already imported
> Workers are being
> Exported jobless.

Hue to hold

> Both
> That morning
> Equally lay
> In leaves
> Kept for
> Another day.

Slant of light

> Growing gloom
> Once at none
> When it comes
> Its echoes fade
> Chalked
> On the sidewalk
> Helpless in such
> Matters.

Get points. Get More.

> Portable pursuit adjustable
> Cash credit check debit
> Step-through design
> Transfers attempt
> Smooth transition.

All my enemies have heard of my trouble

Sweet had become a Marine by accident. After being arrested for driving while stoned, he dropped out of college during his first semester, was evicted from his apartment and soon found himself back in Nebraska, living with his mom. There he met a girl who invited him to go with her back to Fort Collins, Colo., where she attended school. Sweet went. Six months later the girl pledged a sorority and announced she was moving in with her new sisters. "I didn't know what to do," Sweet told me. "So I ended up getting drunk one night and told myself that I should join the Air Force. I showed up in the morning to join the Air Force, and they were closed. So I walked next door to the Marine recruiting office and signed the paperwork." A year and a half later, Sweet was carrying a machine gun through the streets of Fallujah.

Oxen well-laden

Feel the heat
After the boom years
Calm for it is good
To sing praises of the wicked
Expressing alarm over
Assistance rules efforts
Unsearchable to hear their
Cry to save them
His plans perish

(Psalm 144:14)

Who Asks Receives

Economy has shown
Signs of ending
Opinion polls
Committed to demanding
A wholesale withdrawal

Of the law but
Do not judge on
Its promises of prosperity
There are many who
Go in by it

(Matthew 7:7)

A Wayward Gift

Advice is sensible
Risk-free consultant
Architect of adaptive
Management changing
Mediator of the new covenant
For by it the elders
Obtained testimony
Considering
The outcome of their conduct

(Hebrew 11:2)

When He Rose Up

Much remained to be done
Most likely to break the mould
Floundered partly
For inward investment
In spite of solid long
Term growth prospects

He found them
Sleeping from sorrow

(Luke 22:45)

Kiss

When the Passover must be killed
Reduce their exposure
To high yielding assets
Judas signs off
Contradictions with fervent desire
A rubber with
Swords and clubs should be
Considered the greatest

(Luke 22:49)

2.2 The War Ends Here

What thing shall I take to witness for thee?
Unique to the fear of I.E.D.'s is a sense of powerlessness. For Marines, this fear, above every other, rates the most acute. Forgoing tactical formations, they often walk in single file behind engineers with metal-detectors. They overturn suspicious rocks with hooks affixed to bamboo stalks. They mark every turn with lines of shaving cream or baby powder in the dirt. They travel over rooftops, laying ladders across alleys to cross from house to house. After dark they leave a trail of chemically treated Q-tips that glow under night-vision goggles. And they study every step they take for signed of tampered ground. But despite these precautions, there remains a limit to the degree of safety that vigilance affords, and ultimately it is chance that kills or spares you. This fear – the fear of chance and your helplessness to affect it – is a constant companion to the grunts conducting daily foot patrols across the bomb-littered country of northern Helmand.

Convicted felons

They say
Aging is undesirable bad
Something to be avoided
Questioned by
Investigators in the leak probe
To declassify secrets
But also to pardon

Bala Cynwyd

Ride a bike
Have picnic look
For Easter eggs

Not to have such
Fear to come
To the cemetery

Model of your choice

Against
A deep blue sky
Holding a compass

With a bright star
Shining above her
Like a guide

Destined for
A future contained
In time past

Among the heaps of stone
Glittering smile of its heavens

(Jesaja 11, 1-11)

Unconquerable life

In my end
Is my beginning

The tree has brought forth

Its first fruit
My face lost

In the ashes forever
A small pale lemon
Hanging on its branches
In my beginning
Is my end

Screwed up eyes

Between
The skies, the river and the hills
She had learnt

Not to mourn what
The troubled waters
Had borne away

Mindful
Of the testament of
His heart

But tormented over

The purulent book

(Luke 1, 39-56)

Therefore he made the rampart and the wall to lament
"I can no longer consider you a friend," said the Satyr, "a fellow who with the same breath blows hot and cold."

2.3 Are you comfortable doing business with him?

I am the man that hath seen affliction by the rod of his wrath

A few days later, I accompanied a patrol with another squad, led by First Lt. Matt Perry, during which we were invited into a compound by a young man caked from head to toe with splattered mud. The man Kareem Dada, was building additional walls for his home, which he'd recently inherited from his father. Nearby, as he and Perry spoke, Kareem's 9-year-old brother leaned on a pair of old crutches, shifting his weight from armpit to armpit, adjusting the burden on his single leg. Three months ago, the boy and two other brothers had triggered an I.E.D. while playing in an alley near their house. The blast killed one boy and badly maimed the two survivors, who were taken to Camp Leather-neck for surgery. On the way to see them, racing along the Helmand River, Kareem's parents crashed their car and died.

"Who do you blame?" Perry wanted to know.

"The Taliban," Kareem answered automatically. "I hate them. Look at what they did to us."

As the marines left the compound, they found the third brother, who was maybe 13, waiting outside in a wheelchair. Both of his legs were amputated above the knees. He glared at us with naked loathing. He cursed us in English as we passed.

Back at the base, I asked Perry why he thought the third brother's attitude toward the marines had been so different from Kareem's. The lieutenant held up his hands. Maybe they weren't who they said they were. Maybe Kareem's whole story was a fabrication and they'd been involved in placing an I.E.D. that accidentally detonated. This felt plausible, if disturbing. But then Perry offered another explanation, which seemed to suggest a paradox inherent to any counterinsurgency: "They feel like if we weren't here, bombs wouldn't be in the ground."

2.4 Palm Sunday

Nothing out there
In the dark vast

> Largely silent
> Under pressure
> No credit guarantee
> Decision to grant
> It was taken
> Caretaker
> At the time
> Flexible and adaptive
> Vibrant but
> Death does not require any loan
> The rest split equally
> Act as guarantor
> Extended by
> Risk factors and forecasts

Since the burning bush
Passage measures are
Out of sight sculpted
Hidebound the light
To direct the apostate
Beware
Of the scribes for it
Will come as a snare
On all those who dwell but
The dead are raised
Elbowing each other
To be the first
On the face of
The whole earth

Eyes for they see
Ears for they hear

Apocryphal outlook

Forget the past
The hold-up in progress
Almost next door blood-shot

Red azaleas don't
Dig up the past
Dwell on the past you
Won't see flames salt
In its bones poison of asps
Under their lips
Wet snow and mud for viewing
On cold dark days back home tomorrow

They spoke their word
But you will lose both eyes

Their feet are
Swift to shed blood
Beckett

Reluctant heart it tacked
Toward no one place in particular
Self-entombment triumphs
Abandoned and more flexible
Measures introduced sticking
To the plan scrutinize
Their every action angst

Expected to trigger
Decay of a living being
Encounter the market
Worries that the serpents
Are coming that they will
Crush margins rock-hard
Remediable circumstance
What is more
They seem not
To like themselves very much.

2.5 Between Passover and Good Friday

Vanity (Romans 3:10)

Guilt evil defection and
Contrivance too late
Too soon landslides of years
Sound at morning
Impotent grenades till
The day the car bomb
Exploded disintegrating his body
In waves of heat and gas the sounds

Blossom on sharp needles
Cry out all memories
Battle cries separate peace
It is written
There is none righteous no
Not one

Princes are hanged up by their hand: the faces of elders were not honored

For this our heart is faint
For these our eyes are dim
Our wood is sold unto us

Two Mites

Their gifts into the treasury
Out of their abundance
But when will there things be
Upon another for a Galilean?

Palm Leaves

Martyrdom holding the breath
Pressure of expectations but
He enters Jerusalem with
Olive branches for peace

Crucified
That they may see and believe

Remember, what is come upon us
The centerpiece of any memorial for a Marine is the formal construction of his battle cross. The rifle stuck bayonet down, the helmet set atop the butt stock, the dog tags draped on the pistol grip, the boots placed on the ground. The end result is a movingly personlike assemblage of the dead man's essential gear. What holds it all together is the rifle. Clearly, the rifle is meant to symbolize a kind of linchpin – the singularly vital thing. Yet somehow, it is the boots, their laces neatly lopped and tied, that are most affecting. It is the boots, not the rifle, that most evoke an absence. It is the boots that young marines reach out to touch when they kneel before it all.
(End)

3 Motility Operon Resurfaced

or

There Is No Room For Parasites And Idlers

Not a Fragment

Characters: Erika, Franz, Dieter
(they have not spoken to each other since the peaceful revolution, 1989)
Place: Greenroom of a former State Theatre, Berlin, 2012
Direction:
Never in a crescendo, always
Diffused across various
Themes, this muted chorus of
Discomfort swells when
Opinion cuts too deep. Steady

Flow can serve
To educate, amuse and delight –
But, I would have to add, should
Never come at the expense
Of the subject's dignity:
For freedom's battle once begun,
Bequeathed by bleeding sire to son,
Though baffled oft is ever won.

3.1 The Lottery Ticket That I Drew

Erica: Oh no! Everybody enjoys hearing your stories.
Franz: Thank you. I had to cross that bridge again and again. We tried to get everything in the text across very faithfully. A SPECIAL HAIRCUT. To be quite honest. OR EVEN A MONTH. We were living in a small town. Not OUR TOWN. Stopped in a few.
Erica: REPRIMANDED BY A LOCAL PARTY OFFICIAL. That is good.

Franz: In due course I thought that we need to get adults involved. ALL SPELT IN LOWER CASE. I had blond, curly hair and blue eyes. It's all real. TOUGH SON OVER THE FIELDS.

Erica: Legendary material.   MAJORING IN HISTORY. HUE TO HOLD.

Franz: BOTH...

Erica: ...THAT MORNING...

Franz: ... EQUALLY LAY...

Erica: ...IN LEAVES...

Franz: ... KEPT FOR...

Erica: ... ANOTHER DAY.

Franz: Utter foreignness of which you yourself don't realize. HAPPENED TO LIVE IN OUR BLOCK OF FLATS. It'll be strange for me. GROWING GLOOM...

Erica: ... ONCE AT NONE. Tell me all about it. I DON'T KNOW HOW TO SWIM. Triggered by its references?

Franz: How bacteria sense and swim? THERE YOU GO AGAIN. My grandmother supported our work, sewing the costumes. We documented most of our work, with photos. HIS NAME WAS DIETER. I spent a lot of money on buying the collected works of Ibsen. IT FRIGHTENED ME TERRIBLY.

Erica: ONE AT A TIME. Of course. THE OUTER MEMBRANE. It is not at all well known.
Franz: No, I guess not. Were you happy?
Erica: Was I happy! I am with him all the way.
Franz: I have been preparing for months.
Erica: I'll do my best to help. I'M GLAD YOU'RE TAKING IT SERIOUSLY.
Franz: I guess so. POTENTIAL AS VIRULENCE DETERMINANTS. With all possible speed.
Erica: I was afraid I'd be imposing. THERE IS A NEW CLEANING FLUID ON THE MARKET. How many times do I have to tell you?

3.2 Bones in Whispers

Erica: Let's change the subject. I don't believe it! YOU ARE DESPARATE FOR A ONE-ACT PLAY.
Franz: Don't ask me. I'll tell you the story and then three of us will go down for lunch together. FLAGELLUM-SPECIFIC ANTISIGMA FACTOR.
Erica: I don't care. ROTARIAN, FATHER OF TWO, GOES BERSERK IN BEAUTY PARLOR AND KILLS EIGHT WO-

MEN UNDER DRYERS! Well. My arms are perfect.

Franz: MUCHINA. LIMITS ANTIGENICITY. I don't understand. I am an artist. BUT OH, AT WHAT A PRICE.

Erica: You manifest yourself.

Franz: Or daily entertainment.

Erica: Of course they are always in mourning for somebody.

Franz: Both appeals and threats.

Erica: AND THIS WAS WHY I STAYED ALIVE WHEN MOST OF MY CONTEMPORARIES, THE FRIENDS WITH WHOM I HAD WORKED IN THE PARTY ORGANIZATION, LOST THEIR LIVES BECAUSE THEY WERE REGARDED AS ENEMIES OF THE PEOPLE. Perhaps yet by the time. His memory was playing him false.

Franz: Later he was moved. IT'S PAIN IN A CLOUD…

Erica: … IT BEGINS WHERE…

Franz: … IT ENDS BUILD…

Erica: … WITHIN ME AGING…

Franz: … TEARS REMAIN TO…

Erica: … DESCENT ANONYMOUS. Are you treating me?

Franz: What else?

Erica: I am always optimistic. WOULD NOT MISS IT FOR ANYTHING. We are both invited.

Dieter: Why don't you look over some of this material. It, was incredible, said one lawyer who watched him tearing into a dance. He was really getting into it, stomping his feet, his face was red. He was having a blast.

Erica: All differences are the same.

Franz: It's so true, isn't it?

Dieter: He didn't want to have to defend things that might look bad 20 years later. He wanted to be above reproach, where no one could question his judgment or character. There's an element there that's honorable, but I can't say it isn't divorced from a sense of ambition.

3.3 Either Be Shot or Pulverized

Dieter: BETWEEN THE GREAT MILLSTONES OF LABOR. It started as your game, but I'm taking over.

Franz: I was one of you before you became one of us. FLAGELLATION AND MOTILITY.

Erica: I had access to the files.

Franz: You're bluffing. BEWITCHING EYES! I LOVE YOUR DEPARTING BEAUTY.

Erica: Never mind. SMASH IT, BABY, BEFORE IT SMASHES YOU. Despondent time.

Dieter: What did you know, comrade?

Erica: I knew it from the first time I saw him. I sat him here where you are sitting now.

Dieter: What did he want?

Franz: You louse.

Erica: I know all about you too. EENZY-WEENZY. Duty triumphs over pleasure! And that gives rise to thoughts of pity.

Dieter: I'll cram you full of juicy sweets. YOU ARE SENSITIVE.

Franz: I have been meaning to ask you. I KEEP ASKING MYSELF.

Erica: Me too.

Dieter: Me too. I was always against it.

Franz: I am listening? I AM USING A DIFFERENT NAME, OF COURSE. VENCEREMOS.

Erica: I AM LISTENING! Take note, and weep! ETERNITY. You're not annoyed, are you?

Franz: Shoot from the hip, man.

Dieter: I don't think I'll ever finish my explanation.

Franz: I'll finish it. IN GENERAL: HOLD ON TIGHT TO WORDS! THEN THROUGH THE SHELTERED GATE YOU'LL ENTER...

Erica: ...THE TEMPLE KNOWN AS CERTAINTY.

Dieter: Wait till I tell my family. We devoted all our energy to pursuing those aims. CONTENTION AND CONSPIRACY. HOLDING HER BACK FROM BUILDING HER FUTURE.

Erica: Go on, don't stop. Let me show you. They were honest people who sought no personal gain but were committed to the common good.

Franz: Isn't he a scream! THE WOODS ARE BARE. THE FIELDS DESERTED.

Erica: Some liberties with the story. IN THE INTEREST OF REALITY. Dripping blood. Exhibited without pretty evasions. AND THOUSANDS OF HANDS, RAISED IN APPLAUSE, VOTED FOR THE STRUGGLE...

(Intoning what is now officially the 'European anthem', Beethoven's choral setting of Schiller's Ode to Joy, they could sing: Unser Schuldbuch sei vernichtet! / Ausgesöhnt die ganze Welt!)

Dieter: LET OUR BOOK OF GUILT BE DESTROYED – AND THE WHOLE WORLD RECONCILED, Comrade, come on, join us. It happened 23 years ago! We are free to like or dislike anyone or anything. RICH GUY ON A JET SKI, SKINNY KID WITH GRANDMA AT THE HOJO's POOL. But we must hold our heads up high.

Erica: Mission accomplished. STEPPING OUT FROM UNDER SHADOW OF THE THIRD REICH. Credible explicit goal. DEUTSCHE AN EINEN TISCH. But there are limits to this principle. You don't want a TV critic who decides in advance that all reality TV is stupid, or a theater critic who hates operetta.

Dieter: What's crucial is that whatever a critic's philosophy or taste, whatever he might have written about an artist in the past, he approaches each work honestly, WITH AN OPEN MIND.

Erica: Increased compassion for one's neighbor, for instance, can come from something as easy as encouraging yourself to think of him as, say, a fan of the same local restaurant instead of as a member of a different ethnicity.

Dieter: Economically, the Oder-Neisse line threatened to become a North-South divide of the East-West axis,

WITH ALL THE POTENTIAL FOR ENVY, RESENTMENT, TENSION AND CONTEMPT THAT THAT IMPLIED. Both sides in politics are no more necessarily equally responsible than a hit-and-run-driver and a victim.

Franz: Haha! Stepping out. One, two, three! Sharia mia! CLOSER TO THE MAINSTREAM. Stop the days of apologizing for success at home and never again apologize for Germany abroad. Facts are facts, I agree. Reconciliation sealed. ONCE AND FOR ALL.

(End)

Notes

Decomposition at a Distance on the Record
First version written in October and November 2006, changes during spring and summer of 2007, final correction for publication in October 2007;
translated into English by Daniel Meyer-Dinkgräfe (after Christmas and before end of the year 2008), published in English in IN FOCUS, Cyprus Pen Centre/Armida Publications, Nicosia, vol. 6, No 1: March 2009;
Greek translation by Giorgios Neophytos for ANEF, Greek literary magazine, Nicosia, No 36, March-May 2009;
the German original is published in the yearly COMMUNICATIONS (International Brecht Society), 39/2010;
a scenic reading, co-produced by the National Theatre of Cyprus (THOC), the Cyprus Centre of ITI and the Cyprus Pen Centre, was performed on October 20, 2010 at the National Theatre of Cyprus in Nicosia;
four workshop-productions were the result of a "Brecht-

Notes

Training-Session" with the Professional Theatre Training Program (3. year) at the University of Delaware, January 16. – 21., 2011, at Hartshorn Theatre, Newark, DE, conducted by the author.

The Hard Way Out

Newark, DE, spring/summer 2011; poems translated into Greek by Angela Christofidou and Costas Hadjigeogiou; translation into Chinese by Paul Tseng

Motility Operon Resurfaced

Berlin, November 3-4, 2012

Comments

The remarkable achievement of this collection of poetry is not only that here a German writer has mastered the most subtle shadings of the language new to him, but has also intuited the feelings and sentimental of the citizens of two different continents. The reason for that is simple. The poems bring us a universal message.

Guy Stern (Detroit, USA)

I appreciate Bodin's attitude, his experienced perspective, and his rigorous challenge to the ideas, symbols and gestures that shaped human existence under totalitarian conditions. **Motility** expresses not only for us, who lived and survived this period, the need not to forget, but asks the new generations to be aware: the womb he crawled from is still going strong! The play is exceedingly provocative at a time, where the stark facts of the past seem to be ignored. But it is only on stage, where the "joint act of understanding" can make a difference.

Alla Sosnovskaya (Haifa, Israel)

What an intense scenic poetry! There is no unmediated real and no presence, that is not traced and retraced by what it seems to exclude. The author passionately re-invents, re-embodies, re-inscribes, and re-configures the deformations of Western identity as he experienced them in his home country Germany after WW-II. (...) **De-composition**'s classical moderation in form, that is to say the golden mean, shows a clever aesthetic responsibility, which channels a volcano of questions and demands and organizes their outbursts in the audience. A scenic-reading in Greek at the National theatre in Nicosia won overwhelmingly the hearts and minds of the mostly young 400 spectators.

Glyn Hughes (Nicosia, Cyprus)

For Bodin, the "theatre maker", poetry and events have to be visual, simply to be narrative on stage. (...) **The**

Hard Way Out is a laboratory for political disruption. As in Ancient Greek choruses his theatre investigates the collective narrative for the sake of the present. (...) He reaches from the European civil war in the 20th century to the American identity crisis since 9/11.

Paul Tseng (Taipeh, Republic of China)

Since the USA, or rather the more militant portion of the population, keeps stressing her "exceptionalism" and her being "one nation under God", (the author) tackles the task of pointing at the necessity of judging herself by the ethical values of her Judeo-Christian traditions and aspirations in order to support these grand claims. In other words, the general theme of **The Hard Way Out** is in a way a hypocrisy test.

Klaus M. Schmidt (Salzburg, Austria)

Motility is a text that is suited for the theatre stage as well as for radio, as an opera libretto and as a blueprint for a short film. The image that comes to mind is that of a

senile puppeteer (a grotesquely ancient Honecker or Ul-
bricht) who, despite his age (and even beyond his death)
holds the threads in his hands. At the end of the threads
hang no longer the complete puppets (Erika, Franz, Di-
eter), but "merely" the empty phrases and strange com-
binations of words that moulded "GDR"-bureaucratic Ger-
man in such an absurd way. The hand of the puppeteer is
no longer able to move these threads meaningfully and
intentionally – the hand twitches as if independent, and
the phrases come out completely arbitrarily – in the text
they are marked by capital letters. The characters (pup-
pets) have not been able to separate (completely) from
the puppeteer (the regime) and his threads (not only al-
most manageable in number, as with real puppets, but a
chaotic ball of millions of threads!).

Daniel Meyer-Dinkgräfe (Lincoln, United Kingdom)

To a playwright who suffered under the crushing boots
of oppression, as (Bodin) did, the stage offers an oppor-
tunity to voice opinions one dare not shout on a street
corner or express openly in print. Even the term "play"

connotes something informal, a diversion. Yet, beneath the surface of any play worth the price of admission lurks a universal truth, what W. B. Yeats referred to as "Emotion of Multitude," a sub-text through which the artist speaks to us. Yeats used Greek choruses, Shakespearean shadow-plots, and occult symbols under his surface plots to achieve universality. Haus, too, speaks through choruses as in **Decomposition at a Distance** where, for example, a poet, a collaborator of the state security (Stasi), and Gargantua discuss government policies on procreation, or in **Motility Operon Resurfaced** where "a muted chorus ... diffused across various themes ... can serve to educate, amuse, and delight" as directed in the opening poem.

(Bodin) needs neither shadow plots nor occult symbols to drive his points home. His tools, wit and satire, at least in these two plays, tickle the edges of universal truths that draw an audience in to deeper issues. But **The Hard Way Out**, a chorus in prose and poetry dealing with the impact of the war in Afghanistan on American soldiers, fittingly wears the more serious mask of tragedy. The basic story, narrated in prose by a single actor, stands in stark contrast to the rising and falling waves of lyric verse presented by a 15 voice chorus. A beautifully conceived and executed piece of dramatic writing, with a message that demands our attention, **The Hard Way Out** deserves a hearing on an American stage.

Frederick S. Lapisardi (Brownsville, PA, USA)